WRITE YOUR FIRST NONFICTION BOOK

A PRIMER FOR ASPIRING AUTHORS

HONORÉE CORDER

AUTHOR, *YOU MUST WRITE A BOOK*

WRITE YOUR FIRST NONFICTION BOOK

A PRIMER FOR ASPIRING AUTHORS

HONORÉE CORDER

Designed by Dino Marino, www.dinomarinodesign.com

Paperback ISBN: 978-1-947665-27-9

E-book ISBN: 978-1-947665-26-2

ALSO BY HONORÉE CORDER

- *The Bestselling Book Formula: Write a Book that Will Make You a Fortune*

THE *YOU MUST* BOOK BUSINESS SERIES

- *I Must Write My Book: The Companion Workbook to You Must Write a Book*
- *You Must Market Your Book: Increase Your Impact, Sell More Books, and Make More Money*
- *I Must Market My Book: The Companion Workbook to You Must Market Your Book*
- *You Must Monetize Your Book (September 2023)*
- *I Must Monetize My Book (September 2023)*

OTHER BOOKS & SERIES

- *Business Dating: Applying Relationship Rules in Business for Ultimate Success*
- *Tall Order: Organize Your Life and Double Your Success in Half the Time*
- *Vision to Reality: How Short Term Massive Action Equals Long Term Maximum Results*
- *The Divorced Phoenix: Rising from the Ashes of a Broken Marriage*
- *If Divorce is a Game, These are the Rules: 8 Rules for Thriving Before, During and After Divorce*
- The *Like a Boss* Book Series
- The *Miracle Morning* Book Series
- The *Prosperity for Writers* Book Series
- The *Successful Single Mom* Book Series

SPECIAL INVITATION

Be sure to sign up for instant access to all of the resources and bonuses included in this book:

HonoreeCorder.com/FirstBook

TABLE OF CONTENTS

INTRODUCTION

Dear Reader,

Hello! I'm delighted you've picked up this book. It is going to help you get past any blocks you have about writing your book and will encourage you to finally get it done!

If you're like some aspiring authors, you've been—or are—stuck. It's hard to get started on what seems like a gigantic project: writing an entire book. *Or* you're not sure how exactly to put the pieces together. Or both.

You want to write your first book and need detailed guidance. This is the book for you!

(You might even struggle with imposter syndrome. If that's the case, grab my friend Kris Kelso's book, *Overcoming The Imposter,* and he'll help you work through that.)

My good friend and fellow author (and world-class ghostwriter) Kent Sanders* read my blog post on this topic and said, *"You must turn this into a book! Why have I never seen anything like this before? This sure would have been helpful when I first started writing."*

Hmmm.

It's true, crafting an outline and simply writing a book might come intuitively to some. But most need more than just to "craft an outline and start writing."

You might have these same questions:

- How do I decide on my content and know when it's "enough?"
- What order should the chapters go in?
- What constitutes a chapter (how many subtopics or words)?
- How do I know when I've written enough?

- What do I leave in? What could I save for another book?

This is by no means the definitive book on writing a first book. You might love it; take it and run with it. Or you might look at my suggested *book arc* and not like it at all.

Fair enough. Let's get a few things clear really quick (to make sure this book is for you, and not waste another moment of your time if it isn't).

What this book is: a step-by-step process to write your first draft, following my personal process for writing a book (well, at least one of them).

There are many ways to write a book; this is just one way to write yours.

If you're looking for guidance, the way I wrote a few of my books in the beginning, when I needed to *write about this in this chapter,* write about that in that chapter, you've found it.

What this book is not: the *only* way to write a book.

It is *one* way. In fact, it's a variation of "one way."

There are lots of "write your first nonfiction book" books, and they all provide a process.

I've found that aspiring, first-time authors overthink the process and get stuck when their anxiety levels around "doing it wrong" reach a fever pitch.

Not all of them, okay, none of them, have the time to sort through dozens and dozens of books to identify a workable formula they can apply to their knowledge and expertise to just write the book already.

This book is meant to serve as a guide, a template, you (a very smart person) can use to craft your book.

Once you've done the heavy lifting of designing your outline, guess what? You can move the pieces around until they tickle your fancy.

I've written books and then decided the content way back in Chapter Seven would be better served as Chapter Two.

I rarely write without at least trying to find something to give me some direction. Staring at a blank page with a blinking cursor can be the first stop on the trip to nowhere. But when I have a "do this, then this, then that," I am then able to take it and make it mine.

You might know how passionate I am that just about everyone should write a book. When

I started digging into why lots of folks wanted to, but didn't, it came down to one thing in particular: *they didn't know where or how to start.*

Having a reference guide providing *where and how to start* seemed like a logical book to write. And here we are. Turns out that Kent Sanders is not only a brilliant writer, but he's also a great idea-giver. *Smile.*

What this book *is also not:* a comprehensive guide to writing and publishing your book. I provide a lot of insight here, but I don't teach you about many aspects of the writing process, or where and how to publish your book. I've got a list of great books you can reference for these types of information.

So, let's dive into it, shall we? I'm going to share my process, even as I write this book, to guide you through it. That way, you can see how simple it will be for you. Let's do this!

*Kent was also the catalyst behind *The Bestselling Book Formula: Write a Book that Will Make You a Fortune.* If this is your very first book of mine (Hello! Welcome!), you might want to pick that book up, too.

## CHAPTER ONE

YOU CAN WRITE YOUR FIRST BOOK

You can do hard things.

Writing a book can be a hard thing.

But it doesn't have to be! True: it probably won't be easy, necessarily, but it doesn't have to be so hard you don't do it or loathe the process.

As I sit here, during my daily writing hour, embarking on the process of writing this book, I've got my writing playlist going, a hot cup of joe at the ready, and I'm having a *blast!* I love writing so much. Being an author is just the best—and I want to give that gift to you!

I just made that sound wonderful because it is. But you're reading this book because you want to write a book. You know you need to write it. You've talked about it, thought about it, and penciled out ideas. You've got your "Big Idea": the topic of your book, *the one thing* you must write about, share with the world, and use to catapult yourself, your brand, and your business to the next level. Maybe you've even read *You Must Write a Book.*

But you haven't written it yet. *You're here because you're ready.*

So, let's get you out of cogitation and into action, shall we?

First, you *can* write your book. There are no specific boxes to check, permission slips, consent forms, or authorization needed.

You want to do it, you decide to do it, and you do it.

"Just like that?" you ask.

"Yup."

I'm also particularly excited this morning because yesterday I spoke to a previous business coaching client who has become a dear friend. He wants to write a book, and I get to help. (OMG, YES!)

He said, "I'm ready. Where do we start?" I suggest we start *at the very beginning.*

There are plenty of books on the *when, where, why,* and *how* to write, but I won't leave you hanging. Here are some simple tips to help you get your words on paper.

WHEN

When you write is up to you. My writing time takes place in one hour every morning. Five or six days a week, I come to my desk equipped with a cup of coffee *and* a cup of tea, ready to write. A timer is set for twenty-five minutes (I'm a huge fan of the Pomodoro Technique), and avoiding distraction as much as possible (hey, I'm human!), I write. The timer goes off, and I take a quick five-minute break to refill my cups, and off I go again for another twenty-five minutes.

Suggestion: Identify a regular writing time and block it on your calendar. Your book will be worth developing a consistent writing habit. You'll also probably feel great about the fact that you're ahead of schedule (instead of behind—who likes being behind? Not this gal!).

When you intend to publish your book will inform your writing. I work from a publication schedule, and the very first thing I determine is the target publication date. Once I've set a date, all the other dates (when the first draft is due, when the editor gets the final first draft, etc.) are predicated on that final date.

Suggestion: Commit to your publication date. Yes, even if it is a year (or longer) from today, pull out your calendar and decide on a date. Then, make it immovable. For the most part, I treat my publication dates as if a baby is being born. Why? Because once a baby is coming, it's coming! You can't add in a couple more months of gestation because you didn't get the crib put together.

WHERE

Where will you write your book? Wherever you want! While it's true I prefer my desk, same time, same coffee, every day, life happens. I've written on airplanes, in coffee shops, on my mother-in-law's couch, and on a friend's front porch on Harbour Island. The list goes on.

Suggestion: Figure out where you do your best writing and try to write there as much as you can during your predetermined writing time. However, if you find yourself elsewhere, just write there, too.

WHY

Why write your book? Baby, it's a game changer! I've *never* met an author who said, "Yeah, published a book. Nothing happened. Totally regret it."

Suggestion: Grab this book's bonuses at HonoreeCorder.com/FirstBook. I include a free copy of *You Must Write a Book*. I make a solid case (if I do say so myself) about why you're going to want to write that book.

(You can, also, if you'd like, save a couple of hours of reading and just take my word for it now. *Just sayin'.*)

HOW

Now we're getting down to it. *How* you'll write your book is simpler and easier than you might imagine at first: you're going to write it *one day at a time.* You will write it by staying focused on your desired outcome to write a book and become an author. Finally, you're going to write that thing by following this formula.

(I'm doing my part by being as helpful as possible. Work with me here, okay? Okay.)

SEE FINE PRINT BELOW

Okay, now I'm sure you've done something *really hard* before—earned a degree, bought a house, gotten honey from a beehive without getting stung. I mean, I'm sure you can think of something.

You might have said something after the fact, like, "If I knew then what I know now, it would've been easier." You also might've said, "If I had to do it over again, there's no way!" But here we are, post-event, and you're still alive and kicking. I'm sure we can agree you're glad you did it, right? Yup.

My job with this book is to make it easier (not *easy,* don't get ahead of yourself), plus throw in a huge helping of "I'm extra glad I wrote my book!"

*So, here's the fine print:

- Writing a book is so fun! It is also **hard.** You want to be an author, which means there will be times you'll want to quit, chew off your arm and beat yourself to death with it, and/or run off to South America and never be heard from again. Don't do any of those things. Quitting would be such a bummer (you didn't come this far only to come this far); that second thing sounds extra painful, and, also, you'd be missed.

- There is no *easy*, only *easier*. Again, my job is to provide you with a method you can use that will take some of the guesswork, difficulty, and confusion that can come with the first go-around of anything.

- It will take longer, be harder, and cost more than you anticipated. That's the truth— though no one says it. Only in rare cases is it not difficult to do something as complex as writing a book. Plan for extra time, relax, and enjoy the ride. Getting to the day you launch your book will be a heckuva lot more enjoyable for you (and probably everyone who will be supporting you).

Again, you can do hard things. Writing a book can be a hard thing.

Oh yes, one more thing.

It will be incredibly helpful to adopt the belief that you can write whenever, wherever, and however you find yourself during your writing appointments. (Let's face it: we're not JLo—we can't have pink tulips, vanilla-scented candles, and red M&M's personally delivered to us to "set the mood.")

You'll want to think, and eventually believe, something like this:

Whenever I sit down to write, regardless of what is going on around me, I can focus! The words flow effortlessly from my fingers like water from a faucet. Bonus—it's fun, and I love it!

You might think I'm silly, and that's fine. But I'm the expert. This is my book, and you want to write one. (Right?) Okay, so if you can just go with me on this, I promise you're going to have an easier, better, and more successful trip than if you focus on how complex, hard, and frustrating it might be.

Just as you're maybe a tad skeptical about how great this whole writing adventure is going to be, I'm skeptical you're going to take my word for it. Let's visit with some of my author friends, then, who can help you come around.

## CHAPTER TWO

# THESE AUTHORS WROTE A BOOK
(and so can you)!

If you've been wanting to write a book for a long time and need some inspiration to move you forward, this is the chapter for you!

The stages you'll most likely navigate in the process of becoming an author, which I cover in the next chapter, are common. Meaning almost every aspiring author goes through virtually every stage.

Of course, there are exceptions, but *just in case* you're feeling hesitant to really dive in, you should know what they are and how to navigate them.

Super-fast, here they are:

- **Stage One:** Excitement … "I'm ready!"

- **Stage Two:** Self-Doubt … "Am I being foolish? Writing a book is a lot. I'm not sure I can do it."

- **Stage Three:** Disbelief + Overwhelm … "Maybe I really can't do this; it seems too hard."

- **Stage Four:** The *Aha* Moment! … *"I can do it!"*

- **Stage Five:** Delight … "I did it!"

I'm going to walk you through them in Chapter Three, but first, I want you to find comfort and inspiration in the stories of a few of the first-time authors I've worked with or know personally, as well as some who are a part of my community.

Before I introduce them individually, it is important to note they are all, in addition to now being authors, accomplished individuals. And yes, even they, to some extent, navigated each of the stages as well (which you'll read in some of their stories).

Karen Hunsanger, *Surrounded by Champions*

My book is a series of success stories about remarkable individuals, some of whom faced seemingly insurmountable odds. It's about underdogs and superheroes, relationships, integrity, and courage.

I dreamed for years about writing a book. I was that kid who always had my nose in a book and was writing stories at a young age. But until I retired in 2019, I didn't feel like I had the time to write a quality book.

Of course, I wanted it to be amazing.

I didn't know what I was doing, and I also didn't know how difficult the process might be. I went through *every single stage* Honorée talks about here.

1. Excitement, yes! I was beside myself.

2. Self-doubt. *Who the heck do I think I am? No one wants to hear what I have to say.*

3. Disbelief and overwhelm. *Well, heck, this is bigger than I am.*

4. The Aha moment. *Of course, I can do this! No doubt!*

5. FINALLY, I did it!

My advice is simple because the process doesn't need to be so daunting. This is what I did:

First, hang on to that excitement by reminding yourself what it is going to feel like to publish *your* book.

Second, your experience is gold, and there are always people who can benefit from what you know.

Third, it's okay to take short breaks to avoid overwhelm. Don't take too long, though, and continue to think about how it will feel to finish.

Fourth, find a support group. People who have the same goals can offer immeasurable advice and support.

Last, FINISH! It is a fantastic feeling!

I am now an editor and help other authors with their books. That door would not have opened for me if I had not taken that first step and written my book.

Lucas Marino, *Monetize Your Book with a Course*

My journey as a new author may be familiar territory. I had been a writer my whole life, but I wasn't an author. Sure, I wrote blog articles, website copy, work memos, several official government policy documents, and even a doctoral dissertation. However, I hadn't written My Book (cue the dramatic music!).

Like many authors, I had a pile of partially written manuscripts in a folder on my laptop.

I had ideas. I had plans. But I didn't have My Book!

When the time came to follow through and become an actual author, I knew where to turn. Enter Honorée and her epic publication *You Must Write a Book*. I downloaded that thing in e-book, audiobook, and print! Then, I enrolled in her Publishing Ph.D. course. I finally had the road map and encouragement to get out of my own way. I was excited (Stage One!).

I got to work with Karen Hunsanger as my editor. We made huge strides! Then, self-doubt landed directly in my lap (yep, the dreaded one-two punch of Stages Two and Three at the same time).

Was I writing the best book for my business? Should I publish one of my other books first? Was anyone going to read this thing? Is it taking too much of my valuable time?

I shelved that project and started a new book more aligned with my current business. Yes, I started over. Finishing what I started two years prior was no longer the best decision. I needed to serve my clients today, not two years ago.

At that point, everything clicked. The book flew out of my brain. Before I knew it, I was in the mire of editing, proofreading, designing, and final review. Things were finally … right. I was experiencing the Aha moment, and it was fan-flippin'-tastic.

Several months later, I published *Monetize Your Book with a Course,* and the sense of accomplishment and fulfillment was more than I had predicted.

You've got this. Give yourself this gift!

Brittany Stevens, *Smyrna Spotlights*

I love and live to read. Once the inspiration for my first book came to me, I was so excited. I knew I needed to develop a good writing system to achieve published status. As the saying goes, "How do you eat an elephant? One bite at a time!" I developed a daily writing routine and spent at least thirty minutes writing each morning for nearly nine months. I set my alarm for 4:30 a.m. to write before going to my full-time job. Some mornings I was so excited I woke up even earlier sans alarm!

I have experienced every stage of the writing process. Some days I was on fire. However, on others, I felt overwhelmed and like I didn't move the needle. Looking back, the habit of showing up consistently compounded and eventually turned into a published book.

I have published two books to date. In my first book, I showcased my hometown of Smyrna, Tennessee, in *Smyrna Spotlights: Journey Through Local Smyrna*. I felt inspired to write *Smyrna Spotlights* during the pandemic. I hated seeing so many small businesses shut down globally. My goal was, and is, to inspire people to support local as much as possible, and I shared about many of the iconic, locally owned businesses.

I also published *Smyrna, Tennessee: A Coloring Book*. It is a fun and interactive coloring book for all ages to see how truly special this small Tennessee town is.

My life changed when I became an author. Crossing the finish line to becoming published is one of the proudest, most rewarding feelings of accomplishment. I definitely plan on publishing many more books!

Being an author has opened doors and allowed me to meet some amazing people. I think back to how different my life would look had I not taken the leap. I am so grateful to be a part of such an amazing and supportive community.

Whenever I tell people I'm an author, their expression changes. "You're an author? Awesome! I've always wanted to publish a book." I can't help but smile big each time. It's a truly magical feeling.

John Stange, *Build, Grow, and Monetize Your Online Platform*

Writing books is something I've had the desire to do since I was a child. Even before I could spell, I would dictate stories to my mother and have her write down the words while I drew the pictures. As a student in high school, I made a list of all the things I hoped to accomplish in life, and one of the top items on my list was writing a book.

I was in my mid-20s when I attempted to write my first book. I was serving as a local church pastor at the time, and I was highly surprised by how much criticism came along with that role. I decided to study healthy ways to handle criticism, then share my findings in book form.

I got off to a strong start and successfully outlined the major sections of the book, but I started to lose steam once I got to the halfway point of the project. For months, the unfinished manuscript sat on my computer until I finally got sick of thinking about it and set my heart toward finishing it.

When the book was completed, and I held a printed copy in my hands, I couldn't wait to share it with everyone I knew. It wasn't long or profound, but most people in my life seemed excited to read it and showed me a lot of support. I even convinced our local Barnes & Noble to carry it. They agreed to place six copies of *Words that Sting* in their faith-based nonfiction section. All six copies sold, but comically, they never sent me my share of the profits. I didn't care. I was just happy to see something I had written on their shelves.

Looking back, I can honestly say that writing books has been one of the most worthwhile uses of my time. It's a gratifying exercise that contributes to the growth and encouragement of others while connecting to my overall sense of mission and purpose.

Olivia Lovejoy, RN, *Emotional Triage: A Nurse's Guide to Overcoming Burnout and Compassion Fatigue*

When I decided to start writing my book about burnout prevention for healthcare workers, like any first-time author, I anticipated I would struggle to complete it. I was working overtime shifts at the hospital as a Registered

Nurse during the ongoing COVID pandemic in 2021. I would wake up at 3:30 a.m. before my 5:30 a.m. shift just to plunk out a few inarticulate words onto the page. In the dark hours of the morning, I wondered, Who would even read my words, anyway?

The irony that I was writing a book about healthcare burnout, while actively trying not to become burned out in the process, was not lost on me. The strain of hospital work, in addition to the energy spent clumsily writing my first book, was taking its toll.

You Must Write a Book convinced me that I needed to share my story, even if I didn't have it all figured out. My experiences with emotional burnout and resilience could help someone still struggling. We need to sustain the mental health of our healthcare workers.

I am so proud of the book I have written. It is an honest and vulnerable telling of how to practice self-care while caring for others. I pray it will light the way for someone in the dark.

Jeff Adams, *Content for Everyone: A Practical Guide for Creative Entrepreneurs to Produce Accessible and Usable Web Content*

Why I wrote it: I saw this opportunity to merge my day job, working with companies on digital accessibility, and my creative side as an author and podcaster. I see many creatives producing content that isn't accessible to some people in their audience. I wanted to help creatives, and in turn, hopefully, make more of the internet accessible and inclusive.

One challenge I overcame: It took a couple of revision cycles for me and my co-author to write for the target audience. Discussing accessibility with a company that has designers and developers is quite different from talking with an entrepreneur who likely has little technical expertise. Once I approached it as writing so my husband could understand and take the steps we outlined, it flowed much better because he is that creative.

One cool result: I never thought my day job and my creative side could merge, and I'm really enjoying it. No one sets out to make inaccessible content, and I love witnessing the light bulb go on when someone realizes they can make meaningful changes to include more people in their content. I look forward to a lot more of that because it is very fulfilling to help in that way.

Bambi Corso-Steinmeyer, *Dream Tracking: Track Your Dreams and Transform Your Life*

Writing a book was a lifelong dream for me because reading inspired me, and I wanted to inspire others too. I felt I had something important to contribute to the world, and writing my book allowed me to do just that. It gave me a platform for sharing my knowledge and experience.

Throughout my life, I've struggled with low self-esteem. As deeply as I desired to write a book, my inner critic prevailed. *Who was I to write a book?* I don't have a college degree, I'm no expert, and on it went. A breast cancer diagnosis was my wake-up call—it was now or never. Once healed, I attended a conference on dreams (my passion), where I met multiple authors in the field. I realized most were regular people like me. If they could write a book, why couldn't I write a book too? This revelation gave me the confidence and resolve I needed to complete and publish my book. I now have more self-esteem and confidence than I've ever had.

I received a wonderful, published book review from a prominent dream researcher and author of numerous books on dreaming. It was such an honor.

With any luck, these fantastic stories of authors (who were once aspiring authors just like you) have inspired you to keep reading and follow through on your desire to become an author.

If so, let's roll into Chapter Three, where I'll provide insight into the stages aspiring authors navigate on their journey and an overview of the process.

THE STAGES AND THE PROCESS

How many aspiring authors start to write a book and then abandon their quest? It's hard to say. I'm not sure of the statistics because (a) I couldn't find any and (b) I think 87% of statistics are made up on the spot anyway, so I'm unclear how many people there are who would like to write a book but actually abandon the process. I would guess the percentage of giver-uppers is high.

As you read in the previous chapter, the stages aspiring authors navigate are no joke—they aren't for the weak. A lot of aspiring authors give up because they think it's too hard.

They don't understand they are going to want to give up—that ugly middle is a beast!

Plus, they lack a process to give them enough direction to get all the way to their book launch date.

I don't believe for one second you are weak—but you might be unarmed with the insight and information you need to get to book launch day.

You might have been trying to "wing it" in your book-writing process. Up to this point, you may not have had a process, procedure, or formula to follow.

Add to that a lack of understanding of the stages of writing a book you've got to traverse can mean eventually you might give up.

You may have even thought, *I'm smart*—I mean, you've figured out a complex thing or two in your time, right? True story.

(This is different. Writing a book takes all you've got.)

With this chapter, I'm going to arm you with two separate sets of invaluable information: *The Stages* you'll most likely go through, and *A Process* for writing your first nonfiction book. You'll note I did not say *The Process* because this is just one process—mine—that you can use as a touchstone.

The great thing about understanding *The Stages* and having *A Process* is you can combine your increased awareness with your creativity and desired outcome to create one heck of an awesome book!

Let's start with the stages.

THE STAGES

You can expect to go through each of these Stages. They are perfectly normal, so if you know what they are, you can recognize, acknowledge, and maneuver them like the star you are!

Before I cover them in depth, let me throw in a thought: if you don't think one of them applies to you (save Stages One and Five), jump right on into The Process.

I've seen plenty of folks skip one or all of Stages Two, Three, *and* Four. You don't *have* to doubt yourself, get overwhelmed, or have to stumble through to an *Aha!* You can combine Stage One: Excitement with Stage Four: The *Aha* Moment ... "*I can do it!*" and just do it. Far be it from me to slow your roll with a disempowering suggestion.

- **Stage One:** Excitement … "I'm ready!"
- **Stage Two:** Self-Doubt … "Am I being silly? Writing a book is a lot; I'm not sure I can do it."
- **Stage Three:** Disbelief + Overwhelm … "Maybe I really can't do this; it seems to be too hard."
- **Stage Four:** The *Aha* Moment! … *"I can do it!"*
- **Stage Five:** Delight … "I did it!"

STAGE ONE: EXCITEMENT … "I'M READY!"

You're ready!

I'm going out on the skinny branches to guess this is where you are *right now*.

You've come to the conclusion it's time to write your book. (YAY!)

Capitalize on this moment like your life depends on it. Okay, I might be being a *tad* dramatic. Your life might not depend on it, but there's one life that does: your book's.

While you're chock-full of "I'm gonna be an author!" energy, do these three things:

- **What's your date?** Set a date, about a year from now, as your target publish date.

- **Take action!** Read this book and create your first outline using the formula contained in it.

- **Circle the wagons.** Consider getting additional help by finding a book coach, finding a book writing partner or group, or taking a course—or all three. I recommend my course Publishing Ph.D., which will take you from penned to publication.

STAGE TWO: SELF-DOUBT

I'm not sure how long it will be before some self-doubt creeps in but allow me to do my best to head it off at the pass.

Are you being ridiculous? Probably on occasion. But not about this. If you want to write a book, there are about a million (or at least two dozen) reasons why you should and exactly zero reasons why you shouldn't.

Sure, it's hard—anything worth doing requires an almost daily recommitment. You'll have to carve out time to write from what you already use for other activities. There are other books on your topic, but this is proof of concept!

STAGE THREE: DISBELIEF + OVERWHELM

Did I mention it's hard? I'm the book lady, and I'm here to tell you going from blank page to published book is complicated, exhausting, and at times, dispiriting.

Every time I write a book, at some point, I doubt whether said book is a good idea, worth doing, etc., etc., and so forth.

In fact, in every movie, there's an "all is lost" moment. This is when it seems like the protagonist is *not* going to save the world. They will probably die a horrible death, or they'll have to live alone in a one-room cabin in the woods for eternity. But they persist! A miracle happens (yes, I know there's some suspension of disbelief in this scenario), and the sun sets on a beautiful body of water while a toast is made to the victory.

Did you catch the turning point in the story? *They persist.* When you get to the point where you just don't think you can make the time to write another word, no one will buy your book, or the whole process is a stupid fool's errand (and whose idea was this anyway? *Honorée!*), that's when you downshift into fourth gear and punch it.

Read: you keep going until you hit …

STAGE FOUR: THE *AHA* MOMENT!

When you persist (I'm optimistic, I know you can do it!), there will come the moment when things start to fall into place, and you have a moment of clarity. That moment of clarity will convince you that, yes, you, too, can become an author.

It might be when

- Your writing and the words flow through your fingers like you're getting a download from above.

- You see your cover for the first time.

- Your inner circle of *very* early readers sends encouragement because they liked what they read.

- Or something else. You'll know it when you feel it.

That *Aha* moment is going to carry you sailing into …

STAGE FIVE: DELIGHT. I DID IT!

Recently, as I write this, *Monetize Your Book with a Course* by Lucas Marino (you read his story in Chapter Two) was released.

Lucas, like all the authors I've had the honor of working closely with, was like a kid in a candy store in the weeks leading up to his book's release.

You will feel exactly the same way!

Let's hop in your personal time machine for a moment. Let's visit a time in your life when you did something that you originally considered *very hard* (maybe it was, in your mind, tantamount to being virtually impossible).

Close your eyes and picture it. Was it getting your doctorate? Finishing a marathon? *Not* killing your ex-husband when he cheated with your former BFF? (Just kidding.) Seriously, you have already done at least one incredible thing in your life you originally didn't think you could do.

But you did it.

How did you feel? How did you celebrate? How did those around you acknowledge your success?

My suggestion is that you (a) set a deadline for your goal of writing a book, and (b) create a crystal-clear picture in your mind about how amazing you're going to feel when you hold your book for the very first time.

Really get into that visualization and include getting the first box of books delivered, opening it up, holding up your book and looking at it, flipping through the pages, and reading the back cover. You'll also send an email that you're a published author now, you'll probably post on social media, and you'll update your LinkedIn profile. Maybe you'll even host a book launch party with a few (hundred) of your closest friends and associates. And there will be cake (there should always be cake at a proper celebration).

When you're done picturing how magnificent you're going to feel when your book is no longer just a vision, it is now a reality, you'll be ready to come back to the present moment and dig into the details of writing your book.

I'm ready when you are (and I can't wait!).

THE PROCESS

By no means is what I share in this book the only way to craft a book (I know I said this, but it bears repeating). *It is "a way."*

You can take it, though, and make it yours. Once you have a process (or a recipe, formula, blueprint, or equation), you can customize the heck out of it. Or you can use it "as is." Totally up to you!

The process truly begins with your book's Big Idea. The term "Big Idea" refers to a book concept that is both easy to understand and has a big prospective audience.

The Big Idea of Your Book

The Big Idea is to write about *what stems from what people are coming to you for already.* You're a Subject Matter Expert (SME), and people are asking you about, well, what exactly? I'm a publishing expert and book strategist, so people are always asking me how to write, publish, and monetize their books. So, that's what I write about.

To help you identify what you might want to write about, use this formula:

I help (target population) to do (thing of value), [pick one or both] with <u>or</u> without (differentiating quality).

Here's mine:

I help aspiring nonfiction authors write their books with ease and guidance (and without pain and suffering).

It's no surprise that's what I'm writing about! Once you've identified your *subject,* you'll want to figure out which *topic* to tackle. If you picked up this book because you saw its diminutive size and were encouraged by it, that's by design.

Writing, publishing, and monetizing a book can feel like a staggering undertaking, even with great guidance. (It is, or it sure can be.)

Just like I did with this book, you'll want to tackle one topic or aspect of your subject matter expertise. In so doing, you can make a marked difference in someone's life and/or business.

Here's how you know you have the right Big Idea for your book:

- Talking about it lights you up—it is your true passion. You can't get enough of it. Not only that, but you also transfer your passion to others when you talk about it.

- You talk about it all the time, every chance you get.

- It is what you're known for, and it's what people come to you for when they need help.

- You have a unique perspective, and you can share it in one sentence. Also, you could write more than one book (maybe even a series), even though we're only talking about you writing just one right now.

- Your Big Idea is "commercial," meaning *there's a large (huge!) prospective audience.*

When you meet these criteria, the next step is to ensure you have a big enough prospective audience to make writing about this particular idea worth your time and monetary investment.

The Prospective Audience

It is important to do an analysis of your prospective audience *if* you're specifically focused on making money through book sales and royalties. (You may be solely interested in developing business by gifting your books or publishing them for legacy reasons. If this is you, skip this section.)

If the former describes you, identifying the sum total size of your prospective audience is the first step. Because the most you could ever hope for (in a perfect world) is 1% market penetration, you want the size of your prospective audience to be as big as possible, while still writing a book that has a defined audience. There's no such thing as a book for "everyone," even "general" business or self-help books have a clear-cut reader.

Content that caters to as broad an audience as possible is your best bet.

For example, there are more high school athletes than professional athletes. There are more general dentists than cosmetic dentists. There are dozens of real estate agents for every mortgage broker.

Focus on choosing an audience with a large number of prospective readers. This will mean you won't exhaust your audience quickly.

In addition, choosing to focus on an audience that is either constantly increasing (like parents) or has a decent amount of turnover (new graduates) will factor into your book's success.

Finally, you will want to confirm (and you'll know this at a gut level) that your perspective, through your book, will allow, encourage, and provide the environment for your readers to undergo their own evolution.

If you want more insight and in-depth guidance on this topic, you'll find it in my course Publishing Ph.D. In that course, I also cover every *other* aspect of writing, publishing, and launching your first book.

THE PROCESS

Chapter Three in this process is *an overview of the process.* Here is an overview of the process I'm recommending for you to write your first nonfiction book.

I'll start by describing what goes where and why in a book.

FRONT MATTER

Authors often forget about their book's front matter until very late in the process, but I advise you to think about it at the *beginning.* One, proper planning pays plenty. Two, the front matter is the first place you can begin to optimize your book: commencing the author-reader relationship. I'll go deeper into book optimization in Chapter Seven.

The front matter of a book can include any or all of the following:

- A black-and-white mirror image of the book's front cover

- A second title page

- Copyright page

- Dedication

- Acknowledgments (These can also go in the back matter.)

- Special Invitation (This is where you can invite your readers to get to know you better by offering something of value in exchange for their email.)

- Table of Contents

- Foreword

- Introduction

This is how I structure my front matter (what I include and in the order I use). You can forgo the dedication, acknowledgments, special invitation, and foreword, but the rest are pretty standard for books.

INTRODUCTION

Your Introduction is the reader's first introduction to, well, *you.* Done well, it will spark their interest and virtually compel them to continue reading.

I generally write my book's Introduction twice. The first time is when I'm just starting a book. I *think* I know what I'm going to cover, but as a *plantser* (someone who both plots and writes by the seat of their pants—more on this in Chapter Six), my content often expands or contracts. Then my Introduction needs some finessing, so I come back to it after I've written the entire manuscript to ensure it says what I want it to say.

In your Introduction, be sure to

- Include an introduction to your subject matter.

- Give a sense of what you're talking about and the point of view you're taking.

- Provide an overview of what the reader is going to read and learn, and their potential takeaways.

- Amp up the excitement! End your Introduction in such a way your reader is excited and ready to turn the page and dive into the book.

EIGHT (OR SO) CHAPTERS

While I suggest "eight chapters," this isn't a mandate. Eight is my favorite number; it's also a nice round number you can use as your guide. Ultimately, though, you can have a five-chapter book or a 57-chapter book. Entirely up to you!

I'm sticking to eight chapters in this book, using these topics in each chapter as a guide:

- **Chapter One: Encouragement.** You want your reader to feel like they absolutely can create their desired results. They picked up your book because they want what you have as easily and quickly as possible, without pain and suffering. Chapter One is designed to give them the confidence to keep striving for their goal.

- **Chapter Two: Stories and examples.** Because we find ourselves in others, sharing the success stories of others is helpful. It's likely that Chapter One didn't do the job entirely because *you are the expert,* so your readers will think you're a magical unicorn, and they can't possibly get the same results as mere mortals. This chapter can help them get a better sense that they, too, can be successful.

- **Chapter Three: An overview of the process.** You've figured something out, and this is what you are sharing in your book. This is the instructional part of your book, the meat, and its purpose is to provide what your reader can do, step-by-step, to duplicate your results.

- **Chapter Four: Short formula in the form of an acronym, process, or alliteration.** Your readers will get the best results if they have a simple formula they can *read, remember, do,* and *share.* Take your process and make it a "no-brainer" for your reader.

- **Chapter Five: The Formula in action.** How can they put what they've learned from you into practice? Give them more information so not only will they achieve success, but they can also avoid failure.

- **Chapter Six: Other tips, tools, resources, and ideas.** On your journey, you've probably also figured out or discovered a few additional pieces of information they will find invaluable. Include these distinctions and goodies in this chapter.

- **Chapter Seven: How to get results in the best possible way.** Do you have some additional secret sauce? Pointers for avoiding mistakes or accelerating results? Put them in this chapter, a little of both if you're feeling generous.

- **Chapter Eight: Call to action.** You got 'em fired up in Chapter One, send them off to do great deeds, and, as my friend Jay

Papasan says, *Eat tacos.* Okay, not really about the tacos, but you do want them to feel empowered, inspired, and well equipped to take immediate action. (This can, and may, include eating tacos. Who's to say?)

BACK MATTER

A book's back (or end) matter provides an opportunity for the relationship started in the front matter and the main content of the book to continue outside of the book. I call this *maximization* or *monetization.*

When a reader reads your entire book, chances are they like you and either wouldn't mind knowing or would be excited to know how to engage with you at a deeper level. In other words, what else do you offer that they might want to take advantage of—a companion workbook or journal? A course, coaching program, keynote presentation, or some consulting? Your back matter is your opportunity to let them know what else you've got—and even more importantly, more about *you.*

The back matter of a book can include any or all of the following (or just simply provide an author's bio, including their website):

- Author Notes: I go straight to a book's author notes because I want to know more about the author, and I totally love it when they've written "me" a note (your readers will love this, too). Tell readers something they might not know and include a little about what was happening in your life when you wrote the book.

- Acknowledgments (These can also go in the front matter.)

- Special Invitation (You can put it in the back just in case folks missed it in the beginning.)

- Glossary: In alphabetical order, these are the words or terms used in the book that readers may want to look up quickly.

- Bibliography: This is your comprehensive breakdown of the resources you used, if any, to write your book (or those cited in the book).

- Index: Also in alphabetical order, these are the specialty terms or phrases used in the book, including the page numbers on which they appear, for easy reference.

- Call to Action: In traditionally published books, this leads readers to the publisher's website, maximizing the reader-publisher relationship. In a self-published book, this is the author's opportunity to direct the reader to where they can connect with the author.

I typically only include the Author Notes, Acknowledgments, and Call to Action, but this is your book, and you can include any or all of the additional options.

That's it!

That is the entire outline of how you can, with peace of mind, plan and write your first nonfiction book.

But wait, there's more! I thought seeing two quick real-life examples (besides the one you're reading) would be helpful. I'm fun like that, so you'll find two examples in the next chapter. Come with me; this is getting fun (right?).

## CHAPTER FOUR

MY PROCESS IN ACTION

Just as I want you to be very successful in writing your book (and am aiming to take away as much pain and suffering as possible), I know you'll want to do the same for your readers.

In your book's equivalent to this book's Chapter Three, you'll take what you shared and provide examples.

Whether you use a formula, acronym, alliteration, or something else in your book, you will want to make it simple for your readers to get the most juice for their squeeze. In other words, your readers will need to be able to

- Understand your process, and (this is the tricky part)

- Be able to put it into action without *any interaction with you whatsoever,* and

- Duplicate or exceed your results.

Providing options for putting what you're teaching into practice is going to go a long way toward helping them create a successful end result.

There isn't just one way to write a book, and in fact, there isn't one way to apply "my" formula. Following are two examples, using the same outline process. *And,* one is a real book, and the other is a book I intend to write someday.

Prosperity for Writers

Here's an example using my book *Prosperity for Writers:*

- Front Matter

- Chapter One: YOU Can Be a Prosperous Writer!

- Chapter Two: Prosperous Writers Believe They Can!

- Chapter Three: Your Journey to Becoming a Prosperous Writer
- Chapter Four: Get FAME for Prosperity
- Chapter Five: What is Your Money Story?
- Chapter Six: Practical Practices of Prosperous Writers
- Chapter Seven: Accelerate Your Success
- Chapter Eight: Your Time to Be a Prosperous Writer Is Now
- Back Matter

You can see the correlation between the intended topic of each chapter's content with what I actually used in the book.

To show how simple and effective this process is, I've even outlined an entirely new book idea, even as I write this, using my formula.

I've always had in the back of my mind a book about moving to a new place and knowing how to network and develop new relationships quickly and efficiently. With that in mind …

I'll take *Building a Network in a New City from Scratch* for $200, Alex …

Building a Network in a New City from Scratch

- Front Matter

- Chapter One: Welcome to Your New City!

- Chapter Two: Networking Superstars Meet One Person at a Time

- Chapter Three: One Year from Now, You Will Know Everyone!

- Chapter Four: Learn How to MEET (Make new friends, Expect the best, Extend your network to others, Together everyone achieves more) for Ultimate Success

- Chapter Five: Become a True Connector

- Chapter Six: The Magic 3—Find, Build, Nurture

- Chapter Seven: Each One, Teach One

- Chapter Eight: Build Your Network, Starting Today!

- Back Matter

Okay, I know the title needs work, but it helps to *start somewhere*. By the time I publish it (which could be years from now), it will have an awesome title and subtitle. Promise.

Just in case Chapter Four sets you back in your chair a bit, mainly because you hadn't thought about providing a process or formula, let alone an acronym, I've got you covered.

I know *for a fact* that best-earning books have four common elements, that, when you know them, can be applied to your book and exponentially increase the likelihood that it, too, is going to be a bestselling (read: best-earning) book.

I share about them in detail in my book *The Bestselling Book Formula: Write a Book that Will Make You a Fortune.*

The Bestselling Book Formula consists of four elements or *keys,* and they are *read, remember, do,* and *share.* What that means is that the book's title, premise, and the formula contained within it are easy to

1. *Read.* Is the book easy to read?

2. *Remember.* Is the book's title or formula easy to remember?

3. *Do.* Is what the book teaches easy to do?

4. *Share.* Is the book's title or formula easy to share?

When you meet these criteria, your book *should* become a bestselling book. A bestselling book *can* have ten or more years of shelf life when it meets the highest quality standard and contains those four keys, combined with some consistent and intentional marketing by the author. To sharpen your knowledge on these topics, read *You Must Write a Book, You Must Market Your Book,* and *The Bestselling Book Formula.*

Now that you've gotten a sense of the process I use, there's no better time than right now to apply it to your book.

Open up a blank document in Word or Scrivener or grab your legal pad and let's put this formula to work for your book right now.

## CHAPTER FIVE

NOW, APPLY THIS PROCESS TO YOUR BOOK

In this chapter, we're going to craft your book's entire first outline. Yes, we.

You've got your blank document, or a blank page and a great pen—and this book. Let's not forget all (or almost all) you need to put in your book is in your head. Let's get it out of your head and onto the page.

You'll want to read through this entire chapter and come back right here, ready to begin.

FRONT MATTER

You'll remember we start with what's in the front matter. The job of the front matter is to start building the author-reader relationship. My term for this is *book optimization.*

Book optimization is like having coffee with a new connection. They don't know, like, or trust you (yet), but during the meeting, you're building rapport, maybe offering a bit of sage advice, with the hope you'll continue your conversation later. You offer to make an introduction, email a beneficial resource, or provide something else you know they need.

You don't need to overthink this, but very quickly, jot down something you would be willing to give to your new connection (in this case, your reader) in exchange for their email address. This will go on your Special Invitation page.

I invited you, in this book, to join my Facebook community *and* to grab this book's bonuses. (What can I say, I'm a giver!) This might be the beginning of a beautiful friendship, or you may simply subscribe to get the bonuses and then hastily unsubscribe.

My intention is that this book and the free gifts I'm sharing will be enough to start a relationship that, without either of them, most likely would not have occurred.

As previously discussed, the front matter of a book can include any or all of the following:

- A black-and-white mirror image of the book's front cover

- A second title page

- Copyright page

- Dedication

- Acknowledgments (These can also go in the back matter.)

- Special Invitation (This is where you can invite your readers to get to know you better by offering something of value in exchange for their email.)

- Table of Contents

- Foreword (I don't believe forewords sell books, and they certainly aren't required. But if you want to have one, who would be the best person to write it for your book? Someone in your field you admire, with whom you have a relationship.)

- Introduction (I talk about this in more detail, below.)

Now you: next to Special Invitation, make a note of what you think you'd like to offer your readers. *Note: you don't have to call it Special Invitation. You can call it whatever you'd like: Book Bonus, Free Giveaway, or something else.*

INTRODUCTION

Since your Introduction is your reader's first introduction to you, you might want to come back to it. As a reminder, I generally write my book's Introduction twice.

Let's get the bones of your Introduction down:

- What's your subject matter?

- What aspect of your subject matter are you talking about, and what point of view are you taking?

- What is your reader going to

  o Read, i.e., are you sharing your experience, stories, and examples, or citing scientific data?

  o Learn, i.e., how will they benefit from reading your book?

  o Take away? i.e., what will they gain and/ or be able to do once they've finished?

- Leave them wanting more—so jot down why they should cancel their day and read your book right now!

EIGHT (OR SO) CHAPTERS

Remember, eight chapters isn't the "right" number—and this isn't the *Write Your First Nonfiction Book BIBLE*. It's a guide, *a primer,* so it should give you exactly what you need to write your book (already!), or more than enough so that you can get your first draft written, then adjust it to what you truly need.

When I first create a new book's outline, I start with an outline of the chapters, then add full bullet points or notes to assist me with expanding on them better.

- **Chapter One: Encouragement.** Tell why your reader can absolutely put the contents of your book into action. *Give at least three examples.*

- **Chapter Two: Stories and examples.** Share your story, and while you're at it, share a few others. Who are people you know who've taken your advice and been successful? *Provide several examples of different types* *of people you've worked with or observed achieving success with your process.*

- **Chapter Three: An overview of the process.** *Outline what your process is and how applying it will work exactly.*

- **Chapter Four: Short formula in the form of an acronym, process, or use of alliteration or overview.** *Take your process and make it a "no-brainer" for your reader.*

- **Chapter Five: The Formula in action.** *How* can they put what they've learned from you into practice? *Give them more information so not only will they achieve success, but they can also avoid failure.*

  o **Note:** This Chapter Five is doing what you want your equivalent Chapter Five to do: get your readers to take action on your advice! *Is it working? I hope so!*

- **Chapter Six: Other tips, tools, resources, and ideas.** *Include insight, distinctions, and any additional goodies in this chapter.*

- **Chapter Seven: How to get results in the best possible way.** Share any additional secret sauce, or pointers for avoiding mistakes or accelerating results—don't hold back! *Put everything else you've got to help your readers in this chapter.*

- **Chapter Eight: Call to action.** *Leave your readers feeling empowered, inspired, and well equipped to take immediate action.*

BACK MATTER

Deciding what goes into your book's back matter is your opportunity for *maximization* or *monetization*. What else do you have to offer or need to create so you can provide an offer in your back matter? *Define what you want to include in the back matter and include time to create any assets you don't already have available.*

- Author Notes
- Acknowledgments (if not in the front matter)
- Special Invitation
- Glossary, Bibliography, and Index
- Call to Action with available assets

This was intended to get you to put pen to paper and outline your book! If you didn't start the process already, take an hour now (or block an hour or even two on your calendar) and pencil out your book's initial outline. You can grab a copy of the *Write Your First Nonfiction Book Journal,* or (and!) grab *My First Nonfiction Book Outline* worksheet (along with other book bonuses) at HonoreeCorder.com/FirstBook.

## CHAPTER SIX

LETTING THE WORDS FLOW

If you got stuck on any part of Chapter Five, that's not unusual. Plus, you might be reading the whole book before taking action. Or both—you might be reading the entire book, *and* you got mentally stuck when envisioning crafting your book's outline.

I have observed many ways aspiring authors get stuck, not only in the writing process but also in the crafting and outlining process. This chapter is meant to foil every last one of them. In addition, I'm going to share some tools and ideas that will make your writing life easier (and more fun). You're going to write your first book like you've done it dozens of times before, and that's going to feel great!

First, let's get you unstuck, then we'll roll you into some fine momentum. The following are some of the things I hear when I'm talking to aspiring authors about why they are stuck or just haven't written their books yet.

"I have to get it right the first time."

By the time you're really ready to write your book, you've got a lot going for you. Not the least of which is that you're probably a total baller when it comes to your work. You've been doing it so long, you can almost do it in your sleep. You see complex problems and can solve them during a workout while watching YouTube videos and answering emails. All before 6 a.m.

Yes, I *know* you are totally competent. So why is writing your book, specifically an outline, giving you pause?

You might be a perfectionist if …

For the perfectionists in the crowd, I encourage you to strive for a grade of a C or even

C+ in the exercise of writing your initial outline, rather than an A.

You can turn a C outline into a B and then an A before you publish. What you cannot do is turn a blank page into an A+ outline. Nor can you write and publish your first book utterly without flaws, on the first try.

Both your initial stab at your outline *and* your initial first draft will require more than three reviews and revisions. (And that's before you send the whole thing over to your editor for more revisions.) Your book is going to receive a lot of love in the form of revisions, reconsiderations, and reexaminations.

Your job, for right now, is to get it out of your head and on paper.

Go back to Chapter Five and fill in what first comes to mind after each prompt. Trust me on this one—you can lean into the process—it will take care of you and your book.

"Who am I, really, to write a book?"

Highly successful people, those who *should* be writing books, often get very much in their heads about the contents of their book.

Enter imposter syndrome. (Dun_dun_duuun!)

This is a big one, and a lot of people struggle with it. (If you don't, skip to the next part. Far be it from me to suggest a problem you don't have and certainly don't need.)

Here's how you know you *must* write a book:

- You want to write a book. Having the desire is enough.

- Someone or many someones have told you, "You should write a book!"

- You've accomplished something cool, incredible, or astonishing, and other people find it fascinating. They ask you about it, and you find yourself talking about it over and over.

- You have a burning desire to help those following your path to get where you are without some of your pain and suffering.

- You want to write a book. Seriously.

The person who would benefit from writing a book is you, and if you picked up this book, you know it, too. (I cover this in great detail in *You Must Write a Book;* feel free to grab a copy, as it is included with this book's bonuses.)

"I don't know what or how to write."

You've got so many options when it comes to writing your book. Here are two:

- You can write it. (You can type it, dictate it, or even handwrite it.)

- You can hire a ghostwriter to write it. (You'll want to do this if you have more money than time, or you recognize that delegating the writing to a competent professional will allow you to stay focused on other business.)

Let's assume you're the writer. You might be wondering what happens after you have an outline. There are a ton of craft books that specifically address *how* to write, and I've got a list for you in the back of this book. For the purposes of this book, I wanted to shine a light on what first-time authors don't know about writing their first book, including *what* and *how* to write their first drafts.

PLOTTERS, PANTSERS, AND PLANTSERS

There are generally three types of writers—*plotters, pantsers,* and *plantsers.*

Those who want to know exactly what they are going to write before they write are called "plotters." If you are generally a detailed person who plans every aspect of your day (or life), this writing style might apply to you. You will plot your manuscript by not only completing the outline I've suggested, but you'll also want to drill it down until it is a complete outline that will guide you through every chapter, chapter heading, and paragraph.

Those who have an idea and generally know what they want to talk about are called "pantsers" (literally, *one who writes by the seat of their pants*). If you're someone who tends to "pants" life, this might also be a great way for you to write. However, please allow my hindsight to be your foresight: might I suggest at least a light outline before you just start writing?

Finally, there are those who combine the two, and they are called "plantsers."

This is me. I'm a plantser. I create a fairly decent outline, and then I start writing. I create my outline, then my subtopics for each chapter, and then I write.

I do this because I know many things will occur to me to include as I'm writing. Topics and subtopics will evolve during my writing time. Last but not least, I have a few folks I send a very ugly first draft to for some initial feedback, even before my kick-ass editorial team swoops in to make sure my content is solid.

When I met Mark Victor Hansen and he suggested I write my first book (which I did: *Tall Order! Organize Your Life and Double Your Success in Half the Time*), I thought that was a super idea. Here's a bit of our conversation:

> » *But Mark, what should I write about?*
>
> » *Do you have a presentation you've given over and over that people like?*
>
> » *Yes.*
>
> » *Write that down.*

Yes, there was more to the conversation, but here's what's important for the purposes of our conversation in these pages:

I didn't overthink it. I just proceeded to ink it.

I pulled out my speech and used the *talking points* as *writing points*. It was all in my head, so what I really needed was a guide, and I was pretty good to go.

You're pretty good to go, too. You already have the knowledge in your head, which you will share with a dose of "You can do it!" Then you'll round it out with some stories and examples, an overview of your process, your formula, and the formula in action. You'll also add other info your reader can use and insight into how they can get great results.

PROCESSES, TOOLS & OTHER HELP

The Time to Write

I have a whole book, *The Nifty 15: Write Your Book in Just 15 Minutes a Day!,* to help you find the time to write your book and make the most of the time you allocate. After committing to writing a book, blocking writing time is the most important decision you'll make in your writing process.

Until you have time to grab a copy and read it, let me give you a solid writing (and general productivity) hack I use daily.

One question I get on almost every podcast I'm interviewed on is *How have you written so many books?*

Before I tell you what I do, let me first tell you what I do not do: I do not write full-time. My time is divided into multiple business interests, and I also have several personal interests. (I have two companies, including my publishing company, I run the Empire Builders Mastermind, I have a bespoke publishing consulting service, I am the founder of Indie Author University (the home of all of my courses), I'm the co-founder of the Empire Builders MasterClass (the home of courses for entrepreneurs with a dozen instructors and growing), *and* I write books.)

To write several books a year, I use the Pomodoro Technique (a time management technique). I set a timer for 25 minutes and focus on writing (it's what I'm doing right now to write this). When the timer buzzes, I take a five-minute break, then repeat.

I write for 50 minutes once a day, five, maybe six, days a week. That's it.

Honestly, my schedule doesn't allow for more writing than that, and that's just fine by me. This year alone, I will write and publish four books and four companion books (three workbooks and an action guide). Yes, all while just writing less than one hour per day.

So, lest you think you need to carve out several hours during your week or take a sabbatical in a foreign country for a year to complete your book (I had one client who did this—didn't write his book, though), you do not. You just need to set up a consistent writing appointment with yourself that you hold inviolate.

Put a regularly occurring appointment on your calendar. Then, when it is time, write. And write. *Just write.*

THE TOOLS TO WRITE

THE ACTUAL WRITING

There are some writing tools you probably have never used (and haven't even heard of) that might be helpful for getting your book written. But I'm going to suggest you stick with what is familiar to you, at least for your first book.

If you get "the fever" (my term for people who write their book, love it, and want to write more books), you may want to explore other options. If you already know you are going to write more than one book, now is the best time to pay attention to how you write most efficiently and effectively. You'll want to identify your ideal system and process and put them in place. Writing more books will be easier and a lot more fun.

Here are the three most oft-used writing software:

- Microsoft Word. I write my books using a template in Word. (I provide this template and detailed instructions in my course Publishing Ph.D.) You can use a simple document, and that will work just fine.

- Google Docs. I hesitate to put this here because the legal fine print is unfavorable (seriously), but it is easy to use and share.

- Scrivener. Scrivener is a beloved writing software, and it has excellent capabilities (you can keep detailed notes and references, move chapters around, etc.). It is also confusing and frustrating until you get the hang of it, and by the time you do, you probably could've just written your first draft. But if you think you're going to write more than two books, get it and also the course Learn Scrivener Fast.

Numerous authors handwrite their manuscripts, and while I do not do that, it is an option you might want to consider. This choice exists and might be good for those who journal regularly and are used to doing lots of handwriting.

EDITING

The editorial process (editing and proofreading) will be the most expensive part of publishing your book. If you want to keep editing and proofreading costs in line, consider using a software program like ProWritingAid or Grammarly. While a human touch is necessary (my manuscripts benefit from the tools I just mentioned and definitely still come back looking like a crime scene with all of those marks!), you can catch a good bit of your mistakes using one of those programs (and there are others, including Microsoft Editor, which is my first line of defense as well).

TECH(NOLOGY)

Most writers I know use a laptop (a MacBook Pro, my choice), a PC, or any number of other options (such as an iPad, *insert other inferior choices here ... LOL*). There is even the Freewrite device, created and used solely for writing.

The choice is yours, and again, allowing my hindsight to be your foresight, you'll want to be sure to

- Save your draft(s) early and often. Use the autosave function on your device, or at least be sure to save every 10–15 minutes and at the end of every session. I've trained myself to save (command + S) every time I finish a thought, every time I refill my coffee, and at the end of every Pomodoro.

- Have a backup. I save to a backup drive every day or two. If your computer crashes or is lost or stolen, you won't have the heartache of losing your book manuscript (not to mention *all of those other files … so many files!*).

- And a backup for your backup. This needs its own section, as it is multifaceted. So here you go:

SAVE EVERY NEW VERSION

Imagine being seven chapters into a ten-chapter book project, only to realize someone else has deleted the entire project. *Poof.* All of your words are gone with the click of a button.

"Confirm you want to delete all files from all devices." *Yes!*

NO!

That happened to me a few years ago—I was 70% done with a book when one of my coauthors clicked *Yes* when I would have preferred they click *No.* Seven hard-won chapters and months of work were gone.

Don't worry because all's well that ends well.

Not for me or those seven chapters. (I hope you're laughing because I'm able to look back on it and laugh today. Then, not so much.) You're the beneficiary of my horrible, terrible, very bad, "Oops, I deleted the file forever" day. You will institute a redundancy policy so fantastic that you will never have this issue. (Please do this so my pain is not in vain!)

I *used to* work with one single file, replacing the old version with the new one. Meaning, when I received a manuscript back from my editor, I just replaced the old version with the new one from my editor, then made more changes. I'll tell you what I recommend in a minute, but here are the challenges with "out with the old, in with the new."

- You won't be able to look back at something you might have deleted upon realizing you wish you hadn't. More than twice, I've deleted paragraphs, references, notes, and even chapters and later wished I hadn't (or that I could un-delete them).

- You don't have anything to compare the new document to if the old one is gone. Being able to look back on previous versions can come in handy—you just won't know when until you're in the moment.

- Anytime you work with another person, be it an editor, co-author, or even a beta reader, you are sort of putting your fate in their hands if you don't save the old version. They could make changes or delete important stuff you might need later.

In your computer, create a folder to house all of your book's documents and files. Keep it simple and name it your book's title. My folder for this project is WRITE YOUR FIRST NONFICTION BOOK. (It is a sub-folder of my HONORÉE CORDER BOOKS folder. If you plan to write more books, having one main folder is helpful and a time-saver.)

In my book's main folder, I have a sub-folder: MANUSCRIPT VERSIONS.

To avoid any problems (like corrupt files, wishing I could go back and see what I've previously written, etc.), I save every version of my manuscript files, like this:

- Write Your First Nonfiction Book v1. When I'm finished with this final first draft of this book, I'll save it "as is."

These subsequent versions are self-explanatory, based on the full title of the document.

- Write Your First Nonfiction Book v2 TO EDITOR.

- Write Your First Nonfiction Book v2 FROM EDITOR. This is the version I use to accept/reject editor remarks. Then I save it as:

- Write Your First Nonfiction Book v3 CLEAN.

- Write Your First Nonfiction Book v4 TO PROOF. I save v3 as a new version to send to my proofreader.

- Write Your First Nonfiction Book v4 FROM PROOF. This one is used to accept/reject the proofreader's marks.

- Write Your First Nonfiction Book v5 CLEAN.

- Write Your First Nonfiction Book v6 TO FORMAT.

- Write Your First Nonfiction Book v7 POST FORMAT CHANGES. After your book is formatted, there is no doubt you'll discover typos and other errors everyone missed. In case you ever would want to publish a new edition of the book, having a completely updated version of the book in Word will make it easier to have it reformatted when the time comes. Your future self will thank you for keeping a clean and updated version of the manuscript.

Yes, you guessed it, some of these versions are exactly the same, or similar, or they *should be*. Like v5 and v6 should be the same, but have two versions of the same file, just in case there's file corruption or any other problem, I've got not only backup versions *on my computer,* but I've also got copies in my email (because I've sent and received them). Every so often, downloading a manuscript version sent through email is a saving grace.

Housing all of these versions in one sub-folder will make them easy to find, and you'll be glad you have them. Eventually, you can delete them to save space on your hard drive if you want (or move them permanently to that backup drive). I don't ever delete anything, *just in case.* But that's me.

In case you're wondering what other sub-folders I have in each book's main folder, here they are:

- [Book Title] Book Bonuses

- [Book Title] Course Files

- [Book Title] Design Files

- [Book Title] Marketing

- [Companion Book Title] Files (with the same corresponding book folders). I generally do a companion to go with each book, such as a journal, action guide, workbook, etc. For this book, you'll find the *Write Your First Nonfiction Book Journal.* Every companion book has the same process, so you'll want to organize those files in the same way as sub-folders from the main book.

Organizing your manuscript and book files for your first book like it's your sixtieth will help you avoid pain and suffering and feel like your author game is tight (because it is!). Handling your book like a pro (like you do everything else in your professional life) will help you to stay positive, productive, and in control of the process.

Which leads us to one last thing:

The Focus to Write

It is helpful to know you will have a lot of competition for your focus when it comes to your writing. Your personal and professional commitments, colleagues, friends, family, and other interests will all compete with your words. Just when you think, *I'm going to get some writing done,* you'll get an email, text, or call that moves your focus. *And that's okay.*

But I thought it might be helpful if I gave you a bit of additional advice when it comes to holding the wolves at bay so you can get the words down.

Yes, this is different from what I've shared before—because this is more about creating boundaries around your writing than simply finding the time and committing to writing. It always seems that once I've made my commitment and declared, "I'm going to write my book for one hour every day!" the Universe giggles and says, "We'll see about that."

The competition for every moment of your time has, up until now, been fierce. You may have been trying to find the time to write your book for years. If you're a busy professional (and I'm guessing you are), your feet hit the floor every morning with every moment of the day already spoken for. You're not alone. With your hands wrapped firmly around this book, I hope you've set your jaw with the determination to *write your book.*

To help you hold firm to your declaration and arm you against finding yourself in the frustrating situation of not writing your book, of waking up six months from now still staring at a blank screen, here is my number one, daily used, key phrase:

I'm on a deadline.

» *Honorée, can you …*

» *I'd love to. However, I'm on a deadline right now. How about after [insert date]?*

» *You don't have any time sooner?*

» *I do not. I'm on a deadline.*

To be fair, I am *always* on a deadline. I usually have three books in process: the one I'm thinking about (in this case, *You Must Monetize Your Book*), the one I'm writing (this one: *Write Your First Nonfiction Book*), and the one I am just about to publish or have just published *(The Bestselling Book Formula)*.

Guess what? The reason I am able to write books continuously is because I continuously communicate that I'm on a deadline. Guess what else? I still do everything else that's important, and sometimes those other things have to wait a while.

It is not the end of the world if I have to wait a few weeks to meet with someone for lunch or coffee.

You want to write your book; that's why you're here with me in these pages. You don't want to drop any other balls in the process. You've calendared, hopefully, regular blocks of time during which you intend to write your book. Stay committed, and when a person or situation comes your way with the intention of derailing you, just say:

I'm on a deadline.

And because you're not a rude, insensitive person, provide information and insight into when you can make time for whatever or whomever it is that wants you. (You're worth it, so trust me, they'll wait.)

As I've shared how I (now) handle every version of my manuscript, there are other insights I want to share that will really help your first book to be magnificent. Your debut as an author, including the process *and* the final product, will seem *au courant* (like you knew exactly what to do, because you did).

FIRST TIME, BEST TIME

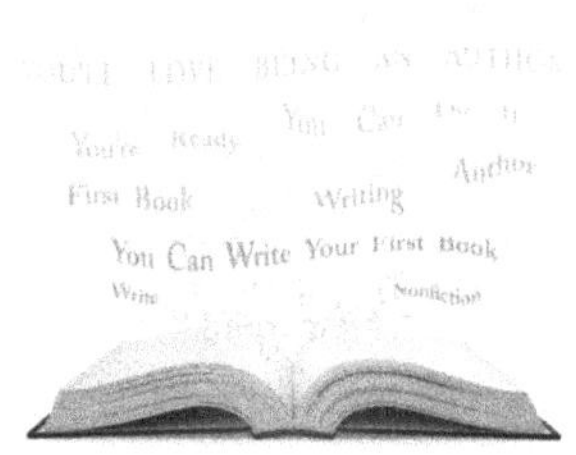

If I knew as a first-time author what I know now, I wouldn't have had to publish my first book *twice*. The first time I didn't know what I didn't know—but I'm fairly smart with a modicum of common sense. I knew I needed a book cover, and that the book's interior needed to be, well, *readable*. And I've been a reader my whole life. Who knew, in just one hundred pages, I could make *So. Many. Mistakes.*

#Facepalm.

IF I KNEW THEN, WHAT I KNOW NOW

There are a few things I wish I'd done better in life, and one of them would be publishing my first twenty books like I've published my last twenty.

This book isn't a comprehensive publishing guide, so you won't find a 187-point checklist to follow (I've got your back, though, with a few book and article recommendations in the book bonuses). This chapter is designed to help ensure your first book will shine with the same polish it would if you had two decades and dozens of books of experience. Which I do—so here are the things I wish I'd known—and what I suggest you do with your first (and every) book.

First: I'd take the time it takes.

I was in *such a hurry* to write my first book. I took Mark Victor Hansen's advice to me, *Take a popular speech, and turn it into your first book,* and I did just that. I wrote it over a weekend and published it not long after that.

Another #facepalm.

This was long before every influencer and celebutante was advertising on social media that they've written nine books, and so can you! "In just thirty days, you too can be an author!" Some even claim they make hundreds of thousands of dollars per year publishing books other people write.

Umm, okay. Settle down.

I want this book, every book I write, and especially your first book, to be so incredible that you're still selling copies and engaging clients a decade from now.

Can we agree there is only a snowball's chance in Hades anyone could hastily write and publish a book that would be the basis for a decade's worth of real success? Okay, then. That brings us to setting an effective timeline. In *You Must Write a Book,* I suggest three possible timelines (100 days, 180 days, or 365 days) with emphasis on the latter.

If you give your book an entire year to bake, you can indeed craft, write, publish, launch, and begin to market it such that it will not only sell a decade from now, but it just might also be the basis of something so big you cannot even imagine it right now.

In *The Bestselling Book Formula,* I talk about how *You Must Write a Book* eventually grew to become what I affectionately call the *You Must Umbrella.* It is a mini empire, with soon a half-dozen books, several courses, and a mastermind. While I produced it fairly quickly in less than 90 days (it was my 21st book, if memory serves correctly), it hits the quality standard I encourage your book to meet.

Plan to take a year—but if you really need your book sooner, then be sure to get the advice of the folks included in this chapter.

Second: I would have realized I needed to spend money to make money.

This isn't just a cliché; it's 100% true. (And don't all clichés become clichés because they are rooted in truth?)

In addition to a year, I'm going to give you a real budget: $15,000. Or, most likely, a bit less.

Before you light this book on fire, let me break it down for you, and then you can tell me if that isn't entirely reasonable. Yes, you can do it for less. Allow me to explain why you might not want to.

With the supposition your nonfiction book will be around 50,000 words, your total publishing expenses, *especially* because you're a first-time author, are going to include the following:

- **A developmental edit.** At eight cents per word, that's $4,000. A developmental edit will ensure your book's arc is complete, that it closes all the loops, and the content will work hard for you (for a decade).

- **A content or line edit.** At five cents per word, your investment is $2,500. Your edit will eliminate most mistakes and ensure a clean read for the reader. A carefully edited book that follows a manual of style followed by a proofread will produce a quality book without typos and misspelled, extra, or missing words. These two passes of your book by professionals will also point out other deficiencies, ensure you give credit where credit is due, and put a true polish on your manuscript, thus allowing it to do the heavy lifting it is meant to do (new clients and higher fees, anyone?). While no book is perfect, and no matter how many eyes you have on a book, something is bound to slip through, having an editor and proofreader will serve to create an enjoyable read for the reader, allowing them to get to know you through your expertise, perhaps turning a prospect into a client. I want to stress that although this isn't absolutely necessary, as a first-time author, you are a prime candidate for these two editing passes because this is your first book.

- **A proofread.** Your proofreading review is going to catch any final mistakes (or 99.9% of them, anyway) and put a high shine on your book, making it as perfect as possible. Your investment here will be between two-and-a-half and four-and-a-half cents per word, so I'll estimate right from the middle at three-and-a-half cents per word at $1,750.

So far, you've invested north of $8,000 US for your book, just for the editorial process, and in the end, it will be well worth it. But what you need to consider investing in your book isn't done yet.

- **Custom cover and interior design.** I recommend using one designer for both your cover and interior design, which allows for continuity in your book's design. You'll note the cover image of this book is used at the beginning of each chapter. I also recommend custom design—you just don't want to see your book cover design on another book! You'll invest $2,000 or more for a cover suite, which includes five covers:

(1) a front cover JPEG for the e-book, (2 & 3) two full covers for paperback and hardcover, (4) a square cover image for social media *and* your audiobook, plus (5) a black-and-white mirror image for the inside beginning of your book. Your book's interior designer will provide a print-ready PDF for both paperback and hardcover, plus an ePub file for e-books, and the investment for all of this is again around $2,000.

- **Copywriting (sales or back cover copy).** Your book needs a book description, also known as *sales copy* (for online retail sales platforms like Amazon, Kobo, and Draft2Digital) or *back cover copy.* You'll want to hire someone who specializes in writing book descriptions. I've got three recommendations, and their fees range from $150 to $600.

- **Miscellaneous (but still important) items.**

  o You'll need to purchase ISBNs, and I suggest buying a block of 10 for $295 directly from Bowker (myidentifiers.com).

  o BookFunnel. At $100 a year, this software will help you distribute books to your advanced reader team; you can also sell books through this platform, and send or distribute free copies digitally.

o Your website. It's a bit much to discuss here, but suffice it to say having a website or page your website readers can visit for more information is a key piece of your overall professional strategy.

Grand total: Your grand total is just over $12,000 *if* you choose to do both a developmental and line edit, and just under $9,000 if you do not. Only you know whether your writing experience rises to the level of needing one pass.

Before I continue, I want to point out that now would be a fantastic time to calculate the value writing your book can *bring to you.*

Third: I might have known my life, business, brand, and income would be forever changed in ways I could not foresee.

With increased brand and face recognition, not to mention the authority your book will bring to the table (this is important, get ready):

You will be even more valuable to the world than you are right now.

What do I mean? As the authority in your space (read: author), you'll be able to command more—25%–50% more—for whatever you do—and *get it.*

- Charge $1,000 an hour for coaching? ***Now you can charge $1,500.***

- Keynote presentations are $10,000? ***You can command $15,000, and your clients won't bat an eye.***

- Consulting gigs are $50,000? ***Yes, you guessed it—you can invoice for up to $75,000 or more—and your clients will gladly pay it.***

"So, you're telling me, Honorée, that when I invest to the tune of, say, $12,500 or so in my book, I'll be able to make 25%–50% more income in my business over the next year?"

No.

I'm telling you that when you invest that amount in your book *once,* you'll increase your income by 25%–50% immediately, and it will continue to grow *forever.*

While your book is a one-and-done proposition, the significance it gives to your life, brand, business, authority, and credibility has an exponential, lifetime impact on your income.

Yes, I'm using "25%–50%" because Alan Weiss says in his book *Value-Based Fees: How to Charge What You're Worth* and *Get What You Charge* (highly recommend, by the way), something to the effect of, "When you have literally *written the book on your area of expertise,* you can charge 25%–50% more than you do today."

But what I really want to say is *the impact being an author will have on your bottom line, over the rest of your life is, in fact, incalculable.*

You simply can't put a price on, in addition to actual book royalty income, the relationships, connections, and doors that will be opened because of your book.

You can estimate what you'll earn, and you'll be able to trace specific dollar amounts back to your book. But if by chance you're on the fence about whether "books are dead" or "the juice isn't worth the squeeze," consider the following:

- The impact of a prospective client or customer noting the fact you're an author. It's a big deal, and it makes a difference in how people perceive you. (Just wait until the first time you're at a party, and you mention you've written a book. Magical.)

- How much less effort it will be to convince someone you are *the expert* in your space—the one they need to hire, engage, or refer. The time it takes to engage a client is compressed, making your time worth more, per hour and per minute.

- How your readers will "feel like they know, like, and trust you" because they've read your book. Do you love your favorite authors and wish you could talk to them? That's how people will feel about *you*.

- The passion you hold for your subject transferring to your readers and *changing their lives for the better.* There's almost nothing better than this.

- The opportunities that will come your way—to coach, speak, consult, engage in a joint venture, or simply (and maybe the best of all) the relationships you'll develop because someone first "met you" in your book.

I rest my case. We, you and I, simply do not know all the miracles, magic, and money that lie on the other side of you writing your book. *But you won't know about any of them, or be in their path, without it.*

So, you're ready, right? *Maybe.*

Note: if the above amounts are giving you a huge pause, I stand by them; however, in this book's bonuses I include some less expensive alternatives for professionally publishing your book on a budget.

I needed to get expert advice, insight, and guidance.

Hold on—you're a first-time author. Are you going to do this alone? *Would you try to scale Mt. Everest without a guide?* Yeah, I didn't think so.

This is the one and only time in this book I'm going to do some shameless self-promotion and suggest you invest in my course Publishing Ph.D. It's the course I wish I'd had the day I decided to write my first book. End of promotion.

I also needed everyone I suggest you engage with in this book to produce a quality book. I made every amateur mistake without them. I appeal (and there's a bit more to come on this) to your desire to make a long-term income and impact with your book by restating the need to invest time and money into your book. This is the only way you're going to get the best ROI (return on investment) from both.

I needed to be clear on what was in it for me.

The benefits of writing a book are well known. You can boost your brand, get more business, and become the go-to expert. You'll be one of the cool kids (authors are the coolest of the cool, *obviously*), and you'll be the life of every party.

What I didn't know before I became an author is what I wanted *from* the book. It turns out the answer was *more clients and equally more revenue*. Get clear on what's in it for you.

One more thing: define the job of your book *before* you write it. A book designed to get you more speaking engagements will have different content (as well as optimization and maximization) than a book designed to get people to sign up for your email address.

Clarity on what's in it for you, as well as the heavy lift the book should make, will help you craft it effectively.

Get Great Advice from <u>Experts</u>

I talked about your investment earlier in terms of cost. I want to talk now about how to ensure your book is the best quality it can be. I'll also share how working with an editor, graphic designer, proofreader, copywriter, and just maybe a book and publishing strategist (that's me) will exponentially and dramatically multiply the quality of your book—and everything that happens after that.

Before I do that, however, allow me to say a few words on crowdsourcing input about your manuscript, book title, or cover design: *please do not do this.* Don't do it to your book or yourself.

Why?

Here's the truth: you want to get input from people who really know, the experts. Your Facebook friends don't know what you're really asking when you say, "Here's my book title; what do you think?" Your question is really, "Is my book title going to compel someone to buy and read my book and ultimately become my client?"

While it is tempting to get excited and share your book with *everyone* and get *everyone's* input, insight, and thoughts, you and your book will be best served if you work on it in a hush-hush environment. The only input I gather is from my inner circle of trusted publishing professionals who really know what they are talking about.

Incorporate the Four Cornerstones of a Professionally Published Book

My first goal when publishing a book is not to sell a million copies (that's my second goal). My first goal when publishing a book is to *publish it such that it is indistinguishable from a book that has been traditionally published.* Those folks in New York, Chicago, and LA hold a high bar for books—and theirs is a standard I strive to meet and exceed.

To run with the big guys, a book has to have the same look, feel, and read they do. Here are the boxes your book must check in order to fit in (and stand out) among its peers:

The cover has to be *awesome.* Yes, I know "awesome" is nebulous, so here are some pointers:

It must look like the other books in your genre, and, when possible, just a tiny bit better. Think: so compelling that someone wants to pick it up, flip it over to read the back cover, buy it, and read it (preferably all on the same day). You'll want to hire someone who specializes in book cover design, who understands the difference between RBG and CMYK (color modes, each used for different formats), and who can produce a clean, clear cover design (not muddy or "self-published looking" (I know you know what I mean!)). You want your book to not only fit in, but you also want it to stand out. You'll want to study the other books in your category, the ones your book will sit next to on bookshelves and online. Make notes of the common design elements and themes, colors, and images.

The back cover needs excellent copy (more on that shortly), a professional photo of you with a short bio, the main category of your book, the price, a barcode, and maybe a testimonial or three. Fire up your favorite online book retailer and check out the covers of books that are selling well after at least a year (check publication date and sales rank … anything under 30,000 in the Amazon store is a great place to start).

As we've discussed, a custom cover will cost around $2,000, but again, before you balk, consider how much clients pay to work with you. One terrific cover can bring new clients *en masse*, making investing in a quality cover a sound investment. As soon as you decide (officially) to write your book *and* you have a working title, engage a designer armed with the research you've done on what you'd like your book cover to look like. The design process takes time, and just like the writing process, you won't want to rush.

You'll want a next-to-flawless read. This means hiring a professional editor and working with them to put your manuscript in order (both in the *right* order and together in such a way it guides and supports your reader). The relationship you develop with your editor can be priceless, as they see your manuscript through different eyes and a distinct set of lenses. A great working relationship will mean a great book. Be sure to find someone who shares your vision, understands your book's purpose, and, when possible, your sense of humor.

Your proofreader will make your final manuscript a smooth read, and it will simply sparkle. They will catch what's been missed and make those final, subtle suggestions that can really make a difference! They'll also ensure consistency in your content and be the last safeguard against mistakes.

Quality editors and proofreaders are in high demand, and you should seek to engage them at least three months before you plan to finish your manuscript. A common mistake I see is that aspiring authors want to write their first draft and *then* find an editor. This is a big mistake, and I promise you'll love knowing you've got a great team waiting for you and your book (the accountability is helpful, too). I have always found my editorial team through personal recommendations, and that's what I recommend you do. Just be sure that what you're hiring them for is their full-time profession.

Interior formatting is mega-important. Clean formatting in an easy-to-read font is a must. You can do a basic format of your book by using a free tool Draft2Digital provides; however, if your budget allows, engage a custom formatter to add in special effects (such as the beginning of chapter graphics, icons to drive home your point in certain sections, or even space to do exercises or a summary of your chapter). You won't regret having custom formatting, especially because you can *optimize* and *maximize* the book. If the goal of your book is to develop new business, I highly suggest investing in quality, custom formatting to enhance the knowledge and expertise you share in your book.

Optimize in the Front Matter and Maximize in the Back Matter

The front and back matter are additional important elements, almost as important as the main content of your book. We've talked about what goes where, but we haven't talked about why.

As promised, I'm going to ensure you understand that in the next and final chapter, Chapter Eight: Write Your First Nonfiction Book … *Now.*

What's important to note here is when you send your final manuscript to your book's cover and interior designer, you'll want to include your book's front and back matter content as well.

You don't need to have the opt-in page or email responder ready, but you'll want to at least know what the URL is—as of the first draft and this writing, HonoreeCorder.com/FirstBook isn't ready to go, but I've identified it, and I have a short list of tasks to complete as soon as the book is with the editor. (You can feel free to check it out because, by the time you're reading this, it will be ready!)

Oh, you'd like my list of tasks? Happy to share. Here you go:

- Create URL: HonoreeCorder.com/FirstBook.

- Create the reader bonuses.

- Create an email response with the reader bonuses (and make sure the links work).

- Double-check tags work to include new subscribers on the regular email list.

Your book description converts prospective buyers to readers. Also known as *sales copy* or *back cover copy,* your book description helps your prospective reader understand what the book is about—and you'll want to *for sure* engage a pro to write it for you! Great copy converts a prospective reader into a reader at a higher rate than even an awesome cover, so fork over the few hundred bucks it takes to have an expert help you *sell your book.*

Your copywriter will need some or all of the following: your book's title and subtitle with a two-sentence, "in your own words" overview of your book, the Table of Contents (with one to two sentences about each chapter), and your long bio.

Note: your book, written in your voice, should sound like you (right?). Your book description *will **not** sound like you,* and it shouldn't. The job of sales copy is to sell. *Please don't make the mistake of taking the sales copy you pay for and "making it sound like you."* That is a mistake I see authors making. Let the copy do its job, okay? Okay. *smile*

These four cornerstones: **custom cover and interior design, editing and proofreading,** and a fantastic **book description** will allow your book to compete with others in your genre—and win! Prospective readers (and clients) won't know it's self-published because it will be so professionally published. They will be not only impressed you're an author but also that your book is so well done!

The Order of Operations & Other Insights

I see first-time (and sometimes seasoned) authors making mistakes when it comes to when to do things and in what order.

In publishing several hundred books over the years, I've made almost every mistake (and discovered many others to avoid) in the process.

While this is not an exhaustive list, here are a few things to keep in mind so you can avoid unnecessary pain and suffering:

- **Suggested edits.** When it comes to your edited manuscript, rather than "accept all changes," you'll want to schedule a couple of longer blocks of time (two or three hours, two or three times) to review each suggested edit, one at a time. *You have the final word; you can accept or reject any suggestion (even the ones following the manual of style your editor uses).*

- **Note:** If you make substantive changes (like adding paragraphs, sections, or even chapters), schedule another edit! *Yes, this will be another investment, but just imagine the mistakes that could be overlooked and what they could cost you in the future.* Think of it this way: the adage "How you do one thing is how you do everything" applies to your book, and you don't want your prospective clients to think your sloppy book product is demonstrative of how you'll handle them.

- **Editing precedes proofreading.** *Every. Single. Time.*

- **Proofreading precedes formatting.** *You will want to do a thorough check of your formatted manuscript to find any final corrections or errors.*

- **Give your designer time to be brilliant.** You're investing money into your cover, and design genius takes time (it just does!), so work with your designer and then allow them to work their magic. Once I have a "working" title and subtitle, I send my designer an email with insight and information so he can get started right away (with *months and months* to work on it). Remember: this cover will be some of your future clients' *first* exposure to you—it needs to be incredible.

- **Final file review time.** Give yourself time to review your final book files and make any corrections well in advance of publication. I print out the formatted manuscript and read it out loud while I walk around with highlighters and sticky notes to mark any mistakes or corrections (and I do this again with a proof copy of my book). Many authors are still writing their books a week or two before they publish. This, in my opinion, leaves no room for error (or the correcting of errors). *There's no need to rush; plan to receive your final files weeks ahead of your official book launch date.*

This final note gets its own paragraph: **No rushing. Take your time.** Seriously, I mean it. (I'm smiling on the inside.) If you think you need six months, give yourself nine or even twelve to write and publish your book. Allow additional time for your designer to craft a book cover that makes you emotional when you see it (this is a thing). Allow additional time for your book content to "rest"—so you can come back to it with fresh eyes and a rested brain. Allow additional time for *life to happen* (because it will), and still meet your deadline with a full night of sleep and a smile on your face.

You're almost ready!

You now know almost everything you need to know (almost!) to write your first nonfiction book, one you'll be proud of, one that will work hard for you. Your book is going to fulfill the vision you have for it, and for that, I'm excited. There is just one more thing I want to share to help you on your maiden author voyage. When you're ready, meet me in Chapter Eight.

## CHAPTER EIGHT

WRITE YOUR FIRST NONFICTION BOOK ... *NOW.*

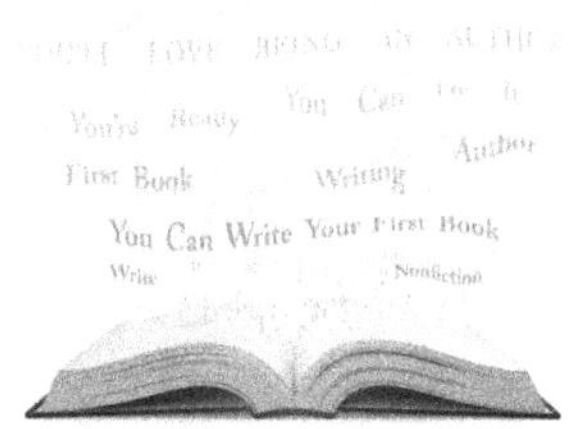

Would it be weird if I put a smile in the chapter title? Yeah, I thought so too, so here it is: :-). I'm being bossy *with a smile* because, let's face it, you picked up this book because you *want* to write your book. You know you *need* to write your book. And you're ready!

I want to provide insight into one more aspect of writing your book before you start actually writing!

I promised to tell you how to take advantage of your book's opportunity to create an author-reader relationship. And I promised to do that by providing clarity around the role of your book's Front Matter and the Back Matter. Just as your book has a job, these two parts of your book also each have a responsibility. So, before we do anything else, let's dive into them because *they are so important!*

Optimize and Maximize Your Book, Your Author-Reader Relationship, and Ultimately, Your Success as an Author

I want you to understand the "why" behind the "what."

Why Optimize? The front matter is your opportunity, as an author, to begin to develop a relationship with your reader. One that will extend far beyond your book. Readers can become clients, and clients can become friends. And it all starts in the front matter. Or, at least, it can!

I include the standard parts of a book in the front matter, such as the introduction and table of contents. In addition, with the intention of creating the opportunity to connect more deeply with my readers, I provide a special invitation for the reader to connect with me, right away, outside of the book.

Internet marketers call the goal of this special invitation to get the "shy yes." Think of it like asking someone out for a first date over coffee. You don't know each other, you don't know whether you might like each other, and you sure as heck don't trust each other yet. Coffee, during daylight hours, surrounded by people, seems like an okay thing to do. Inviting someone to join your email list is the same as asking someone you find attractive to grab a coffee with you.

As an author, you want readers who would benefit from all you have to offer to join your email list. The way to make this happen is through an offer to provide something of value. They give you their email address in exchange for that something of value. You can provide a free report, checklist, or even just access to your email newsletter. The choice is yours, and you're limited only by your creativity.

I want, as will you want, for your readers to join your email list, not just connect on social media. While asking someone to connect with you on social media is a fine idea, you probably don't own any of the social media sites where you would connect. If, for some reason, you are unable to use that social media site at any time, you will also be unable to stay connected. However, you do own your email list, and that's where you'll want to invite your readers to go. If you've read this far and haven't gotten this book's bonuses, and therefore joined my email list, won't you, please? Even if to only get the bonuses—then you can unsubscribe immediately if you'd like or at any time in the future.

However, most people skip right over the front matter, so your carefully planned effort to connect with your readers may be missed entirely when your reader goes right to Chapter One. Happens all the time, but I've got you on this.

Between the front matter and the back matter is the main content—what you're reading right now in this book. You may have noticed I've sprinkled in a few book bonuses. In full transparency, here are the reasons I've done this:

- I want to keep the size of this book *tight.* I know you probably haven't written your book before now because the task seems daunting and overwhelming. Raise your hand if you saw the size of this book and thought, *I can read that! Maybe I can do that!* (I see you. I wrote this book for you!)

- The bonuses are interactive and allow you space to take action on my advice—including them in this book would make the book bigger in both number of pages (see point number one) and in dimensions (most people would rather do the exercises in a writeable PDF or a full-sized workbook). I'm keeping the *information* and the *exercises* separate.

- Finally, I'd love to stay in touch with you via email for several reasons: (a) my emails are legendary for their high content and helpfulness (smile), (b) there's a lot more to know about the art and science of writing a book than I've included here. I share a lot of what else you need to know in my newsletter in easy, bite-sized pieces (so as not to overwhelm you), and (c) I have other opportunities for you to learn from me through (e.g., books, courses, the Empire Builders Mastermind).

Hopefully, my intention to include these bonuses has struck the right chord with you, and you're thinking, *She's got more information, but she's not beating me over the head with it.* That's both my intention and advice. Provide additional information to your readers in a way that *builds* the relationship even while they're reading.

Which brings us to:

How to Maximize! What starts in the front matter (the author-reader relationship) is carried through the main content of the book into the back matter. When someone *gets* to the back of the book, we can assume they've read, enjoyed, and benefited from the book, which can only mean one thing: they would like more!

More information on how they can connect with you. More information on how they can engage with you. More information on how they can engage you. You've probably guessed it: *maximize is another word for* **monetize.**

I believe your reader wants more because they now feel like they know you (at least a little), they like you, and they trust you. At the very least, they want to take the relationship outside of the book. At the very most, they want to know how to get more of what you've got.

They might have already joined your list with the "shy yes" invitation at the beginning, but if they didn't, and they get to the back of the book, they are most likely primed and ready.

You'll want to include what else you have to offer in your book's back matter, in addition to the standard fare. My partner in the Empire Builders MasterClass, Lucas Marino, and I did a video about the Three-Legged Stool. The Three-Legged Stool is how I describe my strategy for launching multiple products (and, therefore, income streams) when I launch a book.

You can find the video on the EBMc YouTube Channel at: https://www.youtube.com/@empirebuildersmasterclass, and search for "Three-Legged Stool."

For example: this book launched with the companion *Write Your First Nonfiction Book Journal* and soon to follow will be the *Write Your First Nonfiction Book Course.* There are strategic and practical reasons for launching them all together (or very close together), including giving you, the reader, everything I possibly can to ensure you succeed.

As you're getting ready to map out your book's content, think about what you want to provide to *your* readers, even before you put your fingers on that keyboard.

Which brings us to:

Putting Your Fingers on That Keyboard, a.k.a., *It's Time to Write Your First Nonfiction Book*

My advice for this chapter, Chapter Eight, is to provide a call to action. So, it makes sense that I will call you to action, even as I encourage you to do the same for your readers.

I hope by now you've been making notes and have a target publish date in mind. In Chapters One and Six, I shared my double-Pomodoro writing process, and I thought I'd give you some additional tips to help you *get your first nonfiction book* written and published by that target date.

Set your writing up to win:

Have a daily appointment to write. My daily writing time is on my calendar, complete with those alarms to keep me focused. I stopped in the middle of writing a note this morning to stay with my schedule. I'm so close to finishing, and I don't want to lose even one minute.

Suggestion: Find another aspiring author and you can hold each other accountable; schedule some writing sprints where you meet on Zoom and then write silently. You know they're going to show up, and therefore, so will you.

Set a project word count goal. The project word count goal for this book was fifteen thousand; however, I'm at almost eighteen thousand without adding in the stories I'm waiting for that go in Chapter Two. I've increased the goal to twenty thousand, without moving my target publication date.

Suggestion: It is always easy to delay the publication of a book if and when you increase your word count, or "life happens." I suggest you avoid this if you can, especially if you're prone to procrastination. I've done some of my best writing when I found myself with a short runway to finish a book project and doubled down on my efforts to meet my deadline (which I know my editorial team appreciated, as did my bank account).

Set a daily word count goal. My daily word count goal is around one thousand words. However, some days I end up with three hundred, and on others, almost two thousand.

Suggestion: When choosing your publication date and crafting your production and publication schedule, give yourself more than enough time so you can always feel a little (or a lot) ahead. Then, stick with your daily writing appointments. This will help you feel confident throughout the process.

Have a countdown! I have eighteen days until this kid is due to my editor. I'm "almost finished" (ROFL—I mean, sort of—giggle giggle), so I'm feeling positive and excited. I still need to tackle a couple of sections from earlier in the manuscript, add in the stories, and then review it several times before it's ready for the first polish. Seeing the days go by, along with your progress, is really going to help you get your book done!

Suggestion: Use the Countdown app so you always know, down to the minute, how much time you have left. Alternatively, you can "Ask Siri," and she'll be happy to tell you at any moment.

Make it public and share your intentions. At the start of 2023, I shared my publication schedule with my assistant (Hi, Holly! You're awesome!), my editor, my mastermind and accountability partners, and my husband (especially my husband!). I didn't declare my intentions publicly, that's not my style, but you might want to because sometimes it's helpful to have that outside accountability.

Suggestion: Share your goal of writing your book with the people around you who matter most to you. Write your goal on a 3 x 5 card and put it on your bathroom mirror, and on a separate one you carry with you. Keep it where you can see it all the time (or a lot!), and just keep working on it until you've done it.

You're going to be so glad you did!

The Single Most Important Section in this Book

Remember: everything I shared in this book is a suggestion. I wrote this book to provide a formula with detailed guidance to help you write your book. You don't have to use each chapter in the way I've suggested, *but you can.* You don't have to put them in the order I have, *but you can.* You don't have to have eight chapters, *but you can.*

If it is easier to work from a recipe (like I do when cooking, for everyone's sake!), then use this as yours.

If you prefer to have a guide but like to get a sense of a process and then make it your own, do it!

You can use this as your handbook, and then "Go rogue!" You can move your content around, write an additional three or five (or more or less) chapters, or really *do whatever you want.*

*It is your book; you get the final word
on just about everything.*

Okay? Okay!

Now, go write your first nonfiction book! You're going to be so glad you did!

AUTHOR'S NOTES

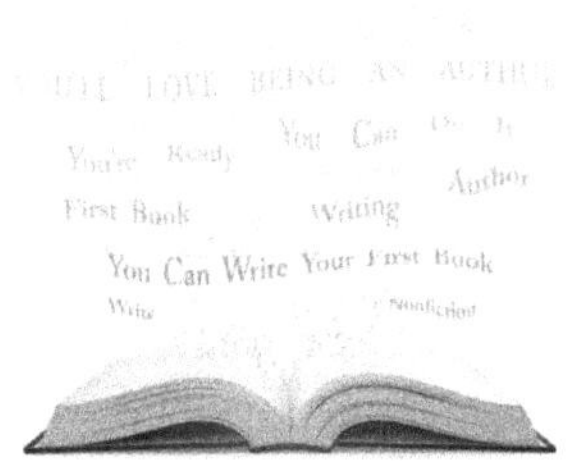

Thank you for reading this book! As I suggested when writing about identifying your book's Big Idea, the idea to write this book stemmed from my newsletter content. This book is another gem of an idea that came through my friend and fellow scribe Kent Sanders, via one newsletter.

"You should write a book about this! It would've been helpful when I was first getting started."

Note taken.

While he was the first to suggest a "newsletter to book" on this topic, I am regularly asked whether I write from a template. Not *per se*, but not a bad idea. Hmm.

Since writing *Prosperity for Writers,* and then *You Must Write a Book,* I've had the pleasure of working nonstop with aspiring authors.

Every party and networking event I attend includes at least one conversation about writing a book. And while *You Must Write a Book* centers more on *the way to write a book* and *what to do with your book,* this one is special in that it provides insight into *how* to get it done.

Because people ask about what book I'm writing at the moment, once I mentioned this one, I couldn't write it fast enough. I have more than a dozen people on my "please send this to me ASAP!" list. It turns out there are a lot of people who want to write a book, and they simply don't know where to start.

With so many people promising to help aspiring authors become authors with everything from courses to done-for-you services (and I have those, too), it seemed to me there was still room for a book like this one.

A book that spelled out a simple, straightforward way to get a book out of one's head and onto the page. A book that didn't require or even allow for pain and suffering, or for a lot of decision-making (and therefore decision fatigue).

A book with a way that eliminated or countered the majority of the reasons people didn't become authors when they wanted to. *All of the ways spelled out by someone with a lot of actual book-writing experience and success.*

As I stuck to my daily double-Pomodoro routine, taking only spare seconds to gaze out of the window in front of my desk, I leaned into my intention for this book. That intention is for this book to turn aspiring authors into authors as quickly and easily as possible—with zero pain and suffering.

The original title of this book was *The Complete Nonfiction Book Formula,* but my research revealed there were several books with that exact or similar title. *Uh oh.* While there's no way to copyright a book title, who wants to create confusion in an already tough book-selling environment? Not this gal.

So with a book title change afoot and a prayer in my heart, I put my fingers to the keyboard. This is what we've got: a fairly short, direct guide that, with every fiber of my being, I hope turns you, the reader, into an author in the very near future.

If you're reading this, won't you please send me an email and let me know whether this book helped and how specifically? Did I provide enough insight and inspiration to compel you to the keyboard? Did I miss anything? Please email me at Honoree@HonoreeCorder.com. I promise if you write, I'll respond. I'm right here waiting.

Happy writing!

Honorée Corder
March 2023

WRITE YOUR FIRST NONFICTION BOOK JOURNAL

Grab *The Bestselling Book Formula Journal* at <u>HonoreeCorder.com/FirstBookJournal</u>.

WRITE YOUR FIRST NONFICTION BOOK COURSE

Get even more guidance with writing your first nonfiction book! Learn more at:

HonoreeCorder.com/FirstBookCourse

BOOKS AND OTHER RECOMMENDATIONS

Other books you'll want to read:

- *You Must Write a Book: Boost Your Brand, Get More Business, and Become the Go-To Expert*

- *You Must Market Your Book: Increase Your Impact, Sell More Books, and Make More Money*

- *The Book You Were Born to Write* by Kelly Notaras

- The Prosperous Writer Book Series: *Prosperity for Writers: A Writer's Guide to Creating Abundance; The Nifty 15: Write Your Book in 15 Minutes a Day; The Prosperous Writer's Guide to Making More Money; The Prosperous Writer's Guide to Finding Readers; The Prosperous Writer's Productivity Journal.* Three of these are with Brian D. Meeks.

- The Like a Boss Book Series: *Write Like a Boss; Publish Like a Boss, Market like a Boss.* All with Ben Hale.

- *The Miracle Morning for Writers* with Hal Elrod and Steve Scott

- Be sure to check out my favorite book recommendations for writers at HonoreeCorder.com/myfavoritebooks.

WOULD YOU KINDLY REVIEW THIS BOOK?

If you've enjoyed this book, please take just two minutes to leave a review where you bought it (and maybe even on Goodreads.com)? I'd be eternally grateful! Thank you!

GRATITUDE

Byron—you're the best husband, partner, and best friend I could ever have. I give a shit, honey.

Renee—thanks for being my sounding board, sane ear, and workout buddy! You're the best, lady!

Kent Sanders—thank you for being the inspiration behind this book! Keep these great ideas coming. *smile*

Writing a book is not done without a magnificent team of people to bring it all together. Mounds of gratitude to my editor, Karen Hunsanger, proofreading ninja, Catherine Turner, design geniuses, Dino Marino and Robert Strasser, and my author buddy and copywriter, Brian Meeks. This book wouldn't be what it is without you!

WHO IS HONORÉE CORDER?

Honorée Corder is an empire builder with more than a dozen six- and seven-figure income streams. She's an executive and strategic book coach, a TEDx speaker, and an author of over 50 books (including *You Must Write a Book*) with over four million books sold worldwide. Honorée passionately mentors aspiring empire builders, coaching them to write, publish and monetize their books, create a platform, and develop multiple streams of income.

Find out more at HonoreeCorder.com.

Honorée Enterprises Publishing, LLC
Honoree@HonoreeCorder.com
HonoreeCorder.com
https://www.linkedin.com/in/honoree/
Twitter: @honoree
Instagram: @empirebuilderusa
Facebook: https://www.facebook.com/Honoree